7 CHAPTERS, 7 DAYS:
How to Live in God's Greatness

Tiffany L. Wade

LOWBAR
PUBLISHING COMPANY

905 South Douglas Avenue • Nashville, Tennessee 37204
Phone: 615-972-2842
E-mail: Lowbarpublishingcompany@gmail.com
Web site: www.Lowbarbookstore.com

Copyright © 2015: Tiffany L. Wade
Printed 2015

Editor: David Pollitt
Content Editor: Calvin C. Barlow, Jr.
Photo: Calvin C. Barlow, Jr.
Graphic and Cover Design Artist: Norah S. Branch

ISBN: 978-0-9862771-7-7
Lowbar Publishing Company
Nashville, Tennessee 37204
615-972-2842
E-mail: Lowbarpublishingcompany@gmail.com
Website: www.Lowbarbookstore.com

For additional information and to contact the author for workshops or seminars:
Tiffany L. Wade
Phone: 615-479-8160
E-mail: t_wade07@yahoo.com
Website: www.buildingyouthpartnerships.com

Scripture references in this book are taken from the King James Version of the Holy Bible, unless otherwise noted.

All rights reserved under the International Copyright Law.
Contents and/or cover may not be reproduced in whole or in part in any form without the expressed written consent of the author or publisher.

7 CHAPTERS, 7 DAYS: HOW TO LIVE IN GOD'S GREATNESS

TABLE OF CONTENTS

Acknowledgement v

Dedication vi

Foreword viii

Preface ix

Chapter 1   It's all about love 1

Chapter 2   We forgive but we don't forget 9

Chapter 3   Don't be the dream killer 16

Chapter 4   Be the overcomer 22

Chapter 5   Be the giver 30

Chapter 6   Find your ultimate purpose 36

Chapter 7   Get to work 43

ACKNOWLEDGEMENTS

I would like to give all the honor and glory to my Lord and Savior Jesus Christ for allowing me to have this opportunity to exercise my gift of writing. I am beyond grateful for the people He has placed in my life to help me grow spiritually and mentally. I thank my parents for their love, patience, and faithfulness. They are very supportive of everything I do, and I thank God for blessing me with the greatest parents in the world. I would also like to acknowledge my friends and family who have been by my side to encourage me to be the best that God has created me to be.

DEDICATION

I would like to dedicate this book to Building Youth Partnerships and all the Youth around the world. I want you all to know that I love you, and I believe you all have the potential to be GREAT in all that you do!! Go conquer the world!!

FOREWORD

By
Drs. Louis & Betty Wade

Having been blessed by God with the gift of our daughter, Tiffany, who truly loves the Lord, we are extremely excited and grateful for her new book, which glorifies His holy name. This fascinating literary work can be easily understood and followed by virtually anyone. The message will not only inspire but encourage readers to want to live in "God's Greatness." Each chapter represents the fulfillment of one's desire to please God. Through the Word of God, Tiffany offers tangible proof on exactly "How to live in God's Greatness."

After carefully reading this book for *seven* days, we found it to be a proven and powerful message for all who believe, or choose to believe, in Jesus Christ. By following the established outline of the book, you will find it to be very easy to read, understand and comprehend. The flow of the narrative will invigorate your thoughts to the extent that you cannot help but want more. You will find that the Holy Spirit is clearly the director of the book; accordingly and most importantly, you can expect your thinking to be *changed* in a way that *you will want to walk worthy* in the presence of God Almighty.

We highly recommend this book to all who desire to live Godly, have a joyful life in Christ Jesus while here on Earth and *are* willing to learn what it takes to do so. It is our prayer that you are strengthened in His Word by this book, and that you are a blessing to others as a result.

Preface

This book will take you on a spiritual journey to enhance your spiritual well-being. You are to read one chapter a day for seven days. Each chapter provides scriptures that are from the King James Bible. After reading this book, you will have a different outlook on your life, and you will be ready to go to the next level that God has for you. There will be a new yearning for you to walk into your purpose and seek God for guidance and live in His greatness. Blessings come to those who seek the Lord and adhere to the Word of God. The first chapter is the beginning of the process of spiritual growth, and it segues into finding your *purpose* to uplift the Kingdom of God. This book will ultimately maximize the potential that God has placed in you to do great works. When you read a chapter a day along with the scriptures, you will be blessed!

It's All About Love

For God so loved the world, that he gave his only begotten Son, that whosoever believeth in him should not perish, but have everlasting life.
—John 3:16 (KJV)

And now abideth faith, hope, charity, these three; but the greatest of these is charity.
—1 Corinthians 13:13 (KJV)

Love is a four-letter word that has more power than we realize. Love is God, and He created us in His image, so we were created to love and not hate. Each day, we should wake up with joy and find a way to show more love and compassion for people we meet and for the people we already know. Our lives are predestined, but along the path that God has set for us He has allowed us to meet people to show them charity. There is a reason why charity is the greatest gift to have and give. When you love someone outside of yourself that is when you begin to live. I never understood why we are so quick to show hate, envy, and pride when love is so much easier to give. Hate is also a four letter word that will destroy you. It will burden you down until you are sick with disease and mental disorders that even doctors can't heal. But, love can overcome any obstacle and illness. It is a known fact that people who have an illness are more likely to survive when they open their heart to give and receive love. I remember when my father was diagnosed with lymphoma cancer, and we were just starting my Building Youth Partnership's Program that summer. I believe that my father became healthier when he took his mind off of his illness and began to show love towards the kids in the program. I began to realize the power of love. I have always heard, like many of you, that love can conquer anything, but I didn't really believe in the power of love until that moment. In the Bible, there are several stories about love that prelude to the love God had for His only Son. When God gave His only Son for us to live eternally and not have to suffer death, He was showing us that love is all about giving yourself to help others live. I know that many of us would not make the ultimate sacrifice of giving up our life for someone that we don't know, but God did. What an amazing sacrifice! We complain when we have to help someone with a simple task instead of being genuine and showing compassion like Christ. Complaining will have you stuck on the side of the road, broke down, and not going anywhere. A grateful heart is sparked through love, and a complaining spirit can't dwell where love is. Let me spell it out to you L-O-V-E is a common word that is tossed around daily; yet, it is so complex and hard for people to really understand. We tell people, "I love you," but do we really know the true meaning of love? It is more than romance, "fire and desire," as the old folks would say. You all know that song Rick James and Teena Marie collaborated on back in the day. Love is deeper than that; it is unconditional, which means that there are no conditions attached. Even when you show love and you don't seem to receive it back, you should still love without an attached condition. While growing up, I was teased and bullied, and I thought that people hated me. It made me feel angry because I never understood why people disliked me. My mother would tell me that I still had to be kind towards the people who didn't like me, and I felt like I didn't. But, as I grew older, I started to realize that when you show love towards people who hate you it will have them confused. They question why you don't hate them back and throw shade at them. The more you show love and mercy towards others, then the more blessings come your way. As I have said, we were created in God's image, and He is love; therefore, we are created to love. Let's take a look at ourselves for a moment. When was the last time you did something for someone else that was genuine and out of love and not for self-recognition? I know it is hard to be genuine in a world that is filled with people who don't care whether you live or die; but in order to overcome the world; you have to create your own space and let people see your light shine through love. Of course, it is not easy to love those who hate and hurt you, but how do you think our heavenly Father feels? We do things every day that are not pleasing to God, but He loves us so much that He shines His light through us so that we can live a fulfilled life. When God created Adam, He loved him enough to create Eve, so that Adam could experience life. Adam began to experience life when he used his ability to love Eve. God knew that it was not good for man to be alone. It was revealed then that humans were not capable of living without someone to love or someone to love them. I can only imagine how Adam may have felt without anyone around to share life with. Companionship is important through life because we all need a shoulder to lean on when we're happy or sad. We spend so much time worrying and arguing over things that don't even matter instead of appreciating and loving what does.

I want you at this time to say out loud, "I THANK YOU LORD FOR LIFE AND THE LOVE YOU HAVE GIVEN ME EVEN WHEN I DON'T DESERVE IT!"

Speaking positive words in the atmosphere brings you positive results. When you begin to speak positive, you see everything in a different light. You're no longer absorbed with bitterness or negativity. However, in order to think positive, you have to have compassion in your heart.

But those things which proceed out of the mouth come forth from the heart; and they defile the man.
—Matthew 15:18 KJV

Whatever is in your heart will come out through your mouth. If you have evil intents and mess in your heart, it can hinder you from receiving the greatest gift God offers, which is love. You can't expect positive results with negative actions. This world we live in may be corrupt, but it is up to you to make your surroundings brighter than the darkest place in this world. You can change the world with one simple four letter word:LOVE. At times, we become so consumed in wanting to be important to the point that we throw darts at the people we feel threatened by. Being important to man should never matter because they could care less of all of your achievements, fortune, and fame. What you do for the Kingdom of God is all that matters. You first have to start with loving someone outside of yourself, and that can open doors for you to become successful. I know we all want to be successful and feel as if we've accomplished something, but how can you take the step to be successful in life when you're selfish, vain, and hateful. Yes, there are people who are successful in our eyes that we know are selfish, vain, and hateful; but they are not successful in life as a whole. You can have a successful career and all the money in the world; but without joy and love that comes from God, how are you really successful? Without love, how can one even exist? People that appear to be successful are sometimes miserable on the inside. So many suicides are committed every day because people don't feel loved. That is why it is important to be that bright light in this dark world because you don't know who is watching you. There are people who look up to you, and you want them to see that you're all about love. They depend on you to guide them to love, so they can be blessed. We can pay it forward with love. It's not always about material things or money; people just need to see that you care. When you show people you care, it will come back to you through others. What you put out in the world will come back. Think about the most negative person you know or knew. I'm sure that everything they see is negative, and they complain about everything that does not matter. Those types of people are bitter from past experiences, and they don't want to love, because they see it as a negative thing, and they are afraid to get hurt. Love should always be a positive element of life because it can overcome any hate. But, in order to love, you have to get over the fear of getting hurt or being used by others. Jesus is a great example of loving those who hurt you. Despite the pain, He endured on the cross; He still loved us enough to give Himself as a living sacrifice so that we could be successful in this life as well as eternally. Once you accept Jesus in your life for real; you will be open to love more, and you won't be afraid of getting used or hurt. You will have a different outlook on life and know that the greatest gift you could ever give someone is love. Even when those you love the most hurt you, it will be easier for you to overcome that hurt because you have the love of Christ in you. I know that loving people is not easy; but in the long run, it can be the best thing you can do. When God see's the love in your heart, He will place people in your life to bless you.

Blessed are the pure in heart:
for they shall see God.
—Matthew 5:8 KJV

A person with a pure heart is loving and compassionate. They are blessed; and if you want to be blessed and highly favored, it is simple: LOVE. When you love on people instead of hating on them, your life will be filled with joy. I can tell you from experience in my life that my success comes from giving love and being selfless. I love who God created me to be, and that has helped me love others and show mercy towards others. I believe that love is somewhere in everyone's heart because God created us that way. However, as people grow up in life and go through chaos, they steer away from the gift of love. Many steer away from love because they have never been shown love from their parents or guardians, so they don't know how to tap into that gift that has already been given by God.

Now, to the parents, it is important to show your children love. The first experience a child has with love is from their parents, so if the parents don't produce it how do we expect the children to do the same? Children model what they see. We have to teach our children or future children how to love, so they can produce it in this world. You can only produce something that you've been given. Even when it comes to romance, parents should show their children that you should be affectionate with your spouse. They have to learn from you, and I know most people want their children to be the best, so show them.

*Train up a child in the way he should go:
and when he is old, he will not depart from it.*
—Proverbs 22:6 KJV

When you teach your children how to love, they won't forget it. They will use what you taught them and apply it to their lives, and then it will ultimately bless them. What happens in a child's life can impact their adult life. If a child does not have parents or guardians who model a compassionate behavior towards others, then they are going to have a hard time developing a compassionate behavior. For example, I believe that a child who is raised without a father figure in their life is going to have a hard time knowing what a father is. You can't model something you've never seen. This is why it is important to be a good model for your children, so they can develop a compassionate behavior. So many people spend their adulthood grieving over situations that happened in their childhood. In order to let go of your past, you have to learn how to first fall in love with Christ.

He that loveth father or mother more than me is not worthy of me: and he that loveth son or daughter more than me is not worthy of me.
—Matthew 10:37 KJV

As stated earlier, love is God, so if you love others more than God, you are not capable of loving others. God is the creator, and we have to put Him first even when it comes to love. When you love God first, He can shine His light on you and show you how to unconditionally love people as He loves you. You will even learn how to cope with your past and forgive those who abused you. Unconditional love is when you can still love someone after they hurt you. Once you learn how to love, you can begin to learn how to forgive. The next chapter gives insight on how forgiving others can be the beginning of healing and moving forward to the next level.

We Forgive
But Don't Forget

*Judge not, and ye shall not be judged: condemn not,
and ye shall not be condemned: forgive,
and ye shall be forgiven.*
—Luke 6:37 KJV

We have all fallen short, and God still forgives us. His grace is sufficient and by His stripes we are healed (Isaiah 53:5). Yet, in this world, people spend so much time angry and bitter because someone abused them mentally or physically, and they don't want to forgive that person. When you can't forgive and let go of that burden, it will keep you down and under attack from the enemy. The devil comes to steal, kill, and destroy (John 10:10). If you keep holding on to the past, how can you expect to live in the present and prepare for your future? How can you judge what another person does to you without evaluating what you may have done to others? It's sad to hear when people say, "God forgives, but I don't" because they don't realize the depth of forgiving someone and moving forward. God has a reason for forgiveness. He doesn't want us to be weighed down with burdens that only He can carry. He did not design us to carry all that extra weight. We were created to praise and glorify God, but you can't glorify God when you're holding onto mess. Unforgivingness destroys everything that God designed for your life. You have to learn how to confess and ask God to help you forgive, so that you can be free from the burden.

If we confess our sins, he is faithful and just to forgive us [our] sins, and to cleanse us from all unrighteousness.
—1 John 1:9 KJV

Once you believe that God can cleanse and forgive you of your sins, it becomes easier for you to forgive others. You begin to realize that you've done a lot of wrong things in God's eyes, and you want Him and others to forgive you, but you must learn how to forgive first.

And be ye kind one to another, tenderhearted, forgiving one another, even as God for Christ's sake hath forgiven you.
—Ephesians 4:32 KJV

Forgiveness is not just about forgiving others but also forgiving yourself. Guilt is another part of unforgivingness from which people suffer. Some people can't let go of what they did to others, and that holds them back from living a righteous and blessed life. I've met so many people who have great potential and talent, but they never reach their full potential because they have so much unforgivingness in their heart. They always walk around blaming others for not reaching success instead of letting go of the bitterness they carry. Bitterness, guilt, and anger take root in people who can't forgive. People who let those negative qualities take root in their life are always miserable and disturbed. They never accomplish anything, and they hate everyone else that is free and successful. Those qualities will have you bound to poverty, stress, depression, and unrighteousness. You will never reach the full potential God placed on your life. There are people out there that could have been scientist to find the cure for *Amyotrophic Lateral Sclerosis disease (ALS), but they were too distracted with their past and not forgiving others. If they would have just come to a place where they could hear from God and forgive themselves or others, they could have reached their full potential. God has placed gifts and talents in all of our lives, but it is up to us to use them. You cannot allow negative qualities like guilt or bitterness to hold you back from exercising those gifts and talents. Those gifts were specifically given to you for a reason because God created you to fulfill a purpose that will glorify Him. Once you break the chains of unforgivingness, you can move forward and create so many great things in this world. On the other hand, people always say, "I forgive, but I can't forget." But, God tells us in His word that He will remove our sins far away from us.*

As far as the east is from the west, so far hath he removed our transgressions from us.
—Psalm 103:12 KJV

He will turn again, he will have compassion upon us; he will subdue our iniquities; and thou wilt cast all their sins into the depths of the sea.
—Micah 7:19 KJV

We have to remember these particular scriptures when it comes to forgiveness. God doesn't hold on to our sins, He forgives and casts it into the depths of the sea. It no longer exists in His eyes. So why do we say I forgive but don't forget? Have you really moved forward, or are you just faking it? If you forgave that person, you will move forward for real, and you'll be so busy living your purpose that you will forget about what this or that person did to you. You won't have time to sit back and dwell on negative things because God gave you a new mind to think about positive things. He will renew your spirit, and you will be free to encourage others and still be positive towards your enemies. That doesn't mean that you have to be best friends with someone, but you'll learn how to have compassion towards that person like Christ. You won't continue to bring up the past, and you'll be free to use every gift that God has given you. Even in relationships, people do or say things that can be hurtful, but the key to moving forward is to forgive each other. God ordained marriage because He knows that a union is powerful, and two Godly people can break so many barriers in this world. I have seen the experience my parents have with forgiving each other and moving forward to create new things together. They are a powerful team of 35 years because they understand the dynamics of how forgiveness is a key note in any relationship. Relationships cannot last if both parties don't know the importance of forgiving and forgetting. Many people don't know the implications of forgetting means that you move forward in your mind, and you don't look back. Even when it comes to abuse you remove yourself from that situation; but in order to move forward in your life, you have to forgive and not look back. When you look back, you will begin to dwell on the abuse, and it will depress you to the point of losing yourself. For example, Lot's wife in the Bible looked back, and she turned into a pillar of salt (Genesis 19:26). God does not want us to bring up the past because it can cause you to lose out on the blessings He has in store for your life. Why waste all your energy on negativity when you can use that energy to be positive. Unforgivingness can cause you to feel like you're constantly drained and unhappy. You will never see the glass as half full or have the strength to move to the next level. From my own experience of thinking back to past hurt, I realized that it slowed me down from reaching my full potential. I thank God daily because I know He has me safe in His hands, and I can move forward with a renewed spirit to accomplish the purpose He placed on my life. We are all destined for greatness because greater is He that is in you, than He that is in the world (1 John 4:4). God wants to use you at your best, not at your worst. He will take the abuse and the evil things that were done to you to refine you, so that He can mold you into His image. Everyone has to experience hurt and pain sometimes in their life because God can work through that so that He can get the glory. Once you get through the test and trials, you have to forgive and forget. You can't look back and blame everyone for the turmoil and the bad decisions you made in your life. People who were abused as a child, and exercise God's gifts, they will tell you that they are able to exercise God's gifts because they forgave and never looked back. I have come to an understanding that forgiveness is a very important aspect in life. It's impossible to please God without faith; and if you can't forgive, you don't have faith in the Word of God. Forgiving someone is having enough faith to believe that God allowed the circumstance to happen to help you to become stronger. If God can forgive that person, so can you. Your faith will become stronger, and you will be refined like gold, then God can exalt you to the next level. God can't take you to the next level when you have unforgivingness in your heart. Don't allow what others have done to you hold you back from the freedom God has given you to use your gifts. By forgiving someone, it allows you to maximize on the greatness that you are destined for. Never let negativity over shadow the good God has placed in you because once bitterness sets in, negativity has won. Once you become negative, everything around you becomes defiled. You will be restless and constantly at war, and you will never have peace. I don't care how much money you have; if you don't have peace in your mind, you will never reach the full potential God has for you. Success should never be about money or status—real success is in Christ Jesus. Forgiveness leads to success, and with success, you will bring forth good fruit. Jesus taught the disciples about forgiveness using the parable about a servant who owed a debt to his master. The servant owed a debt, then he begged his master for forgiveness, and the master forgave him of his debts. However, the same servant was owed a debt by another fellow servant who begged for forgiveness, and the servant did not forgive his debt, instead, he had him thrown in jail. So, the master heard the news and was surprised that his servant had not been merciful to his fellow servant after he was just forgiven of his debt. In the end, the servant was also thrown in jail (Matthew 18:21-35). The moral of this story shows how God forgives us and how we must be merciful in return. If you can't forgive someone else, He will not forgive you. It's as simple as that. Forgive and you will be forgiven. Once you learn how to forgive, you will be blessed beyond what you could ever imagine.

Chapter 3

DON'T BE THE DREAM KILLER

*For where envying and strife is,
there is confusion and every evil work.*
—James 3:16 KJV

A dream killer is what I believe to be someone who despises others who accept their calling and follow their dreams. They allow jealousy to creep in and destroy their own dreams because they're so focused on other's achievements that they neglect their own vision. God gives us all a purpose, but hating on others and seeking to kill their dreams will just kill your dreams in the end. One of my favorite stories in the Bible is the story of Joseph in Genesis chapter 37-41. He was favored by his father Jacob so much that his father made him a coat of many colors, and his brothers were jealous. Joseph also had a gift to interpret dreams. He told his brothers that he had a dream that he would reign over them one day. His brothers became furious and so jealous that they sold him to the Ishmaelites, and they took him to Egypt. When Joseph arrived in Egypt, he was favored by a prominent Egyptian by the name of Potiphar, who allowed him to oversee his house. The Egyptian's wife wanted Joseph to lie with her, but Joseph would not sin with a married woman, so she became angry and lied to her husband and accused Joseph of rape. Once word got back to the master, Joseph was thrown in jail, and that is when he began to interpret dreams. The baker and the butler were placed in the same jail cell as Joseph, and they both had dreams that Joseph could interpret, which helped Joseph make it to Pharaoh to interpret his dreams. Once Joseph interpreted Pharaoh's dreams, he was made ruler of all the land. When the famine came in the land, Joseph's brothers had to go to Egypt and receive help from the same brother they sold. This story teaches several valuable lessons. You can't tell everyone your vision because most of the time people can't see your vision or dream like you can. They thought that they could get rid of Joseph and kill his dream of becoming ruler; but to their surprise, they set him up to walk into his purpose. God will turn what the devil means for evil to something good. Through your pain you sometimes learn your purpose. Don't be like Joseph's brothers and be a dream killer; instead, be like Christ and give people hope to walk in their purpose. When you try to kill people's dream or vision, you are blocking your own blessings because God can't bless someone who has evil intentions. If God blessed you to see another day and you are able to get out of your bed, you have the same opportunity to go after your dreams as everyone else. You can't be bitter or angry towards others who are seeking their purpose. Even, if it appears that others are gaining more acceptance or accolades than you, this does not mean that your hard work is unnoticed. You should never despise small beginnings because God has you right where He wants you to be.

For who hath despised the day of small things?
For they shall rejoice, and shall see the plummet
in the hand of Zerubbabel with those seven;
they are the eyes of the LORD,
which run to and fro through the whole earth.
—Zechariah 4:10 KJV

    He has something greater for you, but you have to be patient and go through the process. For instance, you may be at an entry level position in your field or only have a small amount of money to start your own business—just believe that God is working to take you to the next level. When you start from the bottom, you go through the refining process to be humbled so God can exalt you to greatness, and you can help someone else. It is important to help someone else and not kill their dreams because that same person may have to help you in the future. Joseph's brothers never would have imagined that they would have to depend on him to survive. You never know where people may end up, so don't step in God's way of blessing them because you're just blocking yourself. Small beginnings lead to big things. Tyler Perry, a renowned actor, playwright, screenwriter, director, and producer is a great testimony to people who started from small beginnings. When he started his career in entertainment, it didn't appear that he was going to be whom he is today, but God had a plan to exalt him through his humble beginnings. He was almost about to give up on his passion; and then, God stepped in and opportunities were coming left and right. I'm sure he had many dream killers trying to block him from his purpose; but when he looks back, he realizes those people set him up for a blessing.

Pain can birth some of the greatest work because through pain God can groom you and prepare you. You can look back in your life and think about the dream killers that have tried to block you, and you'll see that you learned something through that experience. One thing I was taught growing up was never give up on the dreams or visions that were given to you because God gave them to you to fulfill. God created us all different for a reason because we all have a unique purpose to live. Having the same job or career may be similar, but your vision for that job can be different. A person can sell cars but have a vision to design a car or own a dealership. If God gives you a vision, it doesn't matter where you start in life; you can't despise starting from the bottom. On the other hand, you can't look at others and despise their small beginnings. It's not even good to speak against someone that may not seem capable of achieving their vision. Speaking against someone is just as bad as doing things to block someone because that's putting out negativity in the atmosphere. One thing to remember is you reap what you sow. If you want to be blessed and highly favored, don't be a dream killer. God wants us to encourage one another and pray for one another so that we can glorify Him. Hating someone will destroy you because you will be so consumed in every step they take that you will lose yourself. Another good example from the Bible is the story of Esther. She was called to save her people for such a time as this. From birth, God chose her, and He orchestrated every step that she took to get to the king. Throughout the story, there were people who tried to block Esther's blessings, but they could not stop God's plan. Haman, a known dream killer in the story of Esther was one of the main people who were close to the king. He tried his hardest to destroy God's people by lying and deceiving the king. Haman even took his time to build the gallows to hang Mordecai; but in return,

Haman built them for himself. As you come to understand, being a dream killer can cause turmoil in your own life. The person you're trying to block will continue moving towards their dreams, they are focused, and they are not worried about you or anyone else who is trying to block them. In order to become successful, you have to be willing to focus on the purpose God has for your life. When you're focused on other people and their accomplishments, you are not going to achieve anything. When you watch the Olympics, you notice that track runners never look back at their opponents. If they do, they will lose the race. You have to stay focused on what God has for you to do. Don't allow Satan to take over your mind and have you focused on destroying someone else's dream. Once you allow Him to take over your mind, you will become bitter towards people who are achieving their dreams. You will be scared to help someone else because you don't want them to do better than you. When you realize that helping someone else can help you or your generations to come is when you have matured enough to receive every blessing God has for your life. Most people who are dream killers don't have a real understanding of their purpose. Having a good understanding of your purpose can free you from hating on other people because you understand who you are. If you don't know your purpose, you don't know who you are.

Where there is no vision, the people perish: but he that keepeth the law, happy is he.
—Proverbs 29:18 KJV

You have to have a vision to fulfill your purpose once you understand your purpose. Don't be the dream killer and lose yourself; instead, be the overcomer and the giver whose light shines throughout the world.

BE THE OVERCOMER

*And he that overcometh,
and keepeth my works unto the end,
to him will I give power over the nations.*
—Revelation 2:26 KJV

The overcomer is victorious and has favor from God. No matter what obstacles may get in an overcomer's way, they always win because the race is not given to the swift but the one who endures (Ecclesiastes 9:11). Giving up is not how God operates in our life, so we shouldn't operate in that manner. Consistency is what gets you to the place God wants you to be. When you give up and quit, you are defeated. The enemy comes to steal, kill, and destroy; and once you've been defeated, He has won. We should never be defeated because we were created in God's image, and we are already victorious in Christ! God has already orchestrated the path for us to get to the finish line and win. But, in order to be an overcomer, you have to be a true believer in Christ Jesus. He came so that we would have eternal life (John 3:16). He suffered for us, so that we could have the Holy Spirit to lead and guide us throughout our life on earth. We are winners! With Christ, all things are possible (Philippians 4:13). If He can bring a dead man back to life, He can bring life to your situation. The overcomer has to have faith to endure their life journey, and they know that God always works things out better than they could imagine. If you seek the kingdom of God first, all things will be added unto you (Matthew 6:33). No matter what obstacles come your way, you will have peace through the storm. Mark 4:35-41 shows how Jesus had peace through the storm when He and His disciples were on the ship. Jesus was asleep throughout the storm until His disciples became frantic and woke Him. He was calm because He knew that the storm would pass and that He was capable of overcoming the storm. However, the disciples did not believe that they could overcome the storm even with Jesus on the ship. That is just like many people today who become frantic over situations that happen in their life. They don't have enough faith to believe that they can overcome any obstacle. Jesus gave you the power to calm the storm because He abides in you. But, In order for Christ to abide in your life, you have to let Him in. God wants all of us to be victorious in all things. Once you began to realize that you are greater and stronger (with Christ) than any obstacle that comes in your life, you can accomplish whatever it is you seek to do. Many times, God allows trials and tribulations to come in your life to shape you and help you grow so that he can exalt you to the next level. If you never go through anything, then you can't give a testimony to someone else.

And we know that all things work together for good to them that love God, to them who are the called according to his purpose.
—Romans 8:28 KJV

The overcomer has this scripture memorized, and they believe that God is working things out for their good. From my past experiences, I know that God always has a better plan, and He will give you the strength to overcome any devil that is trying to hinder you. The greater the obstacles—the greater the blessings! The story of Job is a great example of how God will help you overcome and abundantly bless you. Job was one of God's most faithful and upright servants that had to endure pain. He lost everything in the blink of an eye; but through the test of his faith, he overcame. In the end, Job was blessed with far more than he ever had and was favored by God. Becoming the overcomer is not easy; but once you arrive to that point, you will have peace and joy. When you have joy in the Lord, no demon in hell can bring you down. The devil can try to block you, but God always makes a way for you to get through. I remember starting graduate school, and it was tough at first. I prayed to God to give me the strength to continue and finish. The next thing I knew, I was making 4.0 GPA's almost every semester, and then, I graduated with my Master's Degree. It was a journey, but God gave me the strength to keep going and get to the finish line. The overcomer learns how to pray and communicate with God about everything. Jesus overcame the pain He endured on the cross because He had a relationship with His father. Having that real relationship with God is important, and it's the key to being successful in life. God wants us to lean and depend on him. He knows what we need to get to the next level. Praying is essential to the soul and spirit because God speaks to us when we acknowledge Him. He will direct your paths, and He won't let you stumble. The overcomer meditates on God's word to stay focused on God's purpose for their life. When you meditate daily on God's word, you will begin to find out who you are and the purpose God has for your life. God can only use someone He can guide. He can't guide someone who is not seeking after His word and acknowledging Him. In the Book of Daniel, the servant Daniel faced an obstacle that many of us would have not had the faith to overcome. He was put into the lion's den to die, but he prayed to God to save him, and God heard his cry. Daniel had enough faith to overcome the lions, and he believed that God would protect him. Daniel was an overcomer, and his faith proved that with God's help you can overcome the impossible. While Daniel was in the lion's den, people thought he would have been eaten alive, but God stepped in and showed the people that all things are possible in the Lord. The overcomer knows that, "God will never leave you nor forsake you" (Hebrews 13:5). They know that even when God appears silent that He is still working. When you're a true believer in Christ, you know that you can even overcome death as Jesus did. You will not be afraid to conquer anything! When you learn to be an overcomer, you also learn to become an achiever. You will start setting goals to achieve, and you will be eager to set more goals. When Moses had to flee from Egypt, he ran into several obstacles. He had to make it through the desert and hard labor that he was not use to. Along his journey, he learned how to survive and accept his calling to save the Israelites from slavery in Egypt. God allowed him to go through certain obstacles for a reason. If he did not go through the desert and learn how to survive in that condition, he could not lead his people. Moses was a leader, so he had to overcome many obstacles to be able to lead the people through the desert. God has called many to lead; and with that privilege, there are going to be many obstacles that you are going to have to overcome. So many of us ask God to give us certain gifts and titles without knowing the journey we're going to have to take to get it. You can't focus on what other people are doing or how they're living because you don't know what they had to overcome to get there. Focus on what God has for you and overcome the battles you have to fight within your life. Be the overcomer that can testify how God brought you through, and how He healed you from sickness. God will allow you to go through situations that only He can help you through, so that He will receive all the glory. I am a witness of the miracles of God! He will bring you through and exalt you in His time. Be patient and be the overcomer like Jesus. Throughout His life, Jesus taught us how to overcome temptation and to be righteous. In Matthew 4, when Jesus was fasting for forty days and forty nights in the wilderness, Satan tried to tempt Him by telling Him to turn the stones into bread. Satan tried to get Jesus to surrender to Him by offering Him kingdoms. But, Jesus knew His purpose, and that He already had the power to rule over everything because He is the son of God. Satan thought he could tempt Jesus at a weak point when He was hungry. That's just how Satan works even today, He will tempt you at your weakest point. However, Jesus gave us the strength to overcome the enemy; and if you depend on Jesus, He will help you through that test. Jesus made it clear that man does not live by bread alone but by the Word of God. When you start using God's Word to fight back, the devil will back down, because he has no power. God tells us to seek His kingdom first and His righteousness and He will add everything else. Once you realize that God has given you power and victory, Satan can't offer you anything, but sorrow and heartache. Overcoming temptation strengthens you and allows God to use you for His greatest works. God can't use someone who allows the devil to lead them to destruction; He wants you to be a strong soldier. When a person gets recruited for the military, they have to take tests and go through training, so that when they are deployed they are prepared. It's the same with God; He has to prepare you for spiritual warfare. If you're not prepared to fight, how can you expect to be victorious? God wants us to prepare, by seeking Him through His Word; you can't know the Lord unless you meditate on His Word every day.

For we wrestle not against flesh and blood, but against principalities, against powers, against the rulers of the darkness of this world, against spiritual wickedness in high places.
—Ephesians 6:12 KJV

Be sober, be vigilant; because your adversary the devil, as a roaring lion, walketh about, seeking whom he may devour.
—1 Peter 5:8 KJV

Blessed is the man that walketh not in the counsel of the ungodly, nor standeth in the way of sinners, nor sitteth in the seat of the scornful. But his delight is in the law of the Lord; and in his law doth he meditate day and night. And he shall be like a tree planted by the rivers of water, that bringeth forth his fruit in his season; his leaf also shall not wither; and whatsoever he doeth shall prosper.
—Psalm 1:1-3 KJV

Once you seek His Word, He will equip you to fight in His army, and you will have the power to overcome the wiles of the devil. Satan knows that his time is limited, and that He has no power, but He tries to deceive us into thinking that He has power over us. The overcomer knows that God has all power, and He created us to withstand any obstacle. You overcome through the love of Christ and by forgiving others. You will prosper in all that you do and your leaf will not wither. God will provide all that you need, and He will be with you always. Being an overcomer is not easy, but that's why God gives us the Holy Spirit to guide and comfort us.

Likewise the Spirit also helpeth our infirmities: for we know not what we should pray for as we ought: but the Spirit itself maketh intercession for us with groanings which cannot be uttered.
Romans 8:26 KJV

The Holy Spirit will comfort you and give you the strength to overcome any obstacle. All you have to do is pray and ask the Holy Spirit to help you. Once you overcome obstacles in your life, you won't be afraid to conquer the world. You will have more faith, and you will know that God is always working on your behalf. God wants us to know in all these things that we are more than conquerors through Him that loved us (Romans 8:37). Overcoming is also a key component in becoming a giver. God wants us to share and be selfless without looking for rewards. Overcomers learn how to help others get through tough situations.

BE THE GIVER

Thou shalt surely give him, and thine heart shall not be grieved when thou givest unto him: because that for this thing the Lord thy God shall bless thee in all thy works, and in all that thou puttest thine hand unto.
—Deuteronomy 15:10

Giving is important to God. Being selfless is hard at times, but God blesses those who sacrifice. When you start giving out of your own needs, God notices; and He will give you back everything you sacrificed and more. Jesus is the prime example of giving. He gave His life and suffered the tormented death. He had to bear the cross just so we could live. He knew that we needed a comforter to help us through our life's journey. If He had not given his life we would all be destined for destruction. Being the giver means learning how to love others and giving your life to God, so that He can use you to bring others closer to Him. Once you give your life to Christ, you will want to give more because you know that pleases God. It's an awesome feeling to know that you helped someone else. There is a great example in the Bible from Mark 12: 41-44 of the lady who gave all she had. The lady gave two mites (pennies), and that's all she could give, but Jesus said she gave the most because she gave out of her needs while the others gave out of their wealth. We are supposed to give tithes and offering to God, and He asks that we give ten percent in tithes. Whatever you earn, give God your tithes (tenth percent) first, and you will reap blessings.

Bring ye all the tithes into the storehouse,
that there may be meat in mine house, and prove me
now herewith, saith the LORD of hosts,
if I will not open you the windows of heaven,
and pour you out a blessing, that there shall not
be room enough to receive it.
—Malachi 3:10

The giver will always have what they need and more. God is always in the blessing business! Once you begin to give, you will have a new outlook on life, and you will always look for ways to give.

Give, and it shall be given unto you; good measure, pressed
down, and shaken together, and running over, shall men
give into your bosom. For with the same measure that ye
mete withal it shall be measured to you again.
—Luke 6:38

Growing up, I learned that what you give out, you will get back, whether it's positive or negative. For example, Oprah always gives back to the community, and she never seems to go broke. It appears that she gains more as she gives to others. People who hold on to things never reap the blessings that God has for them, and what they keep is all they're going to get. From my own experience, I noticed when I started giving more; things started going better in my life. The obstacles that I faced weren't as difficult to overcome. It was times that I had nothing to give, but I trusted God, and then gave what I could. However, giving is not always about money, giving your time to do community service is equally important. You have to find time to give back to the community and help those who are less fortunate. Time is just as valuable as money, if not more valuable, so taking the time to help others is pleasing in the eyes of God. Some people give to be recognized by people, and that's not a good intention. When you give, it should be from the heart because God gave His only Son to help us. God wants us to have good intentions towards others, and He knows when those intentions aren't genuine.

Every man according as he purposeth in his heart, so let him give; not grudgingly, or of necessity: for God loveth a cheerful giver.
—2 Corinthians 9:7

He that giveth unto the poor shall not lack: but he that hideth his eyes shall have many a curse.
—Proverbs 28:27

Giving to others should be seen as a blessing, and it should be something that you enjoy doing because God loves a cheerful giver. When you give and complain or when you don't give at all, you will not be blessed. Giving is the key to becoming selfless and having a longer healthy life. Helping someone else makes you feel better because you know that you were an inspiration to someone. Nelson Mandela is another example of someone who was giving. He spent over twenty years in prison because he fought for a good cause to help people in South Africa. God blessed him to live long enough to become the first Black President of South Africa and to see the changes that he and others made. His desire to help others trumped the obstacles he had to overcome to gain freedom. People that give from the heart and have a desire to help others always reach success. You can't be afraid to help and give back because someone is counting on you to help make a difference. Imagine if Martin Luther King Jr. didn't take a chance to fight for African American rights, we would still be separated and treated unequally. If people were selfish all the time, this world would not last one day because everyone needs help from someone. Changes occur through overcoming obstacles and realizing that it's your turn to help someone else. Life is a cycle; and through that cycle, you should learn how to pay it forward. My mom is another person that comes to mind when I think about a giver. She always gave, and not one time did she ever expect anything in return. My mother will give you her last, and she has always taught me to do the same. I continue to see God work in her life through her giving, and all I can say is that she is a blessed woman of God. We should all aim to be the giver and work diligently to help others in their time of need. There are times that God places people in your life for a season to help them and during that season, you may be planting a seed that will sprout to be something great. You never know who you're helping. They may become the President of the United States one day, and they'll always remember who helped them. One thing to remember is you didn't get where you are by yourself. Someone had to help you get there. That's why it's important to pay it forward because helping someone else can allow that person to help the next person. When God abundantly blesses you, He expects you to give. Giving leads to a life full of joy, gratefulness, and happiness. It should put a smile on your face to see the results of you helping someone else. Being selfish leads to a life of depression, it keeps you thinking about your needs or those who are close to you and no one else.

> *My mother always tells me, "The more you help others, the less you worry about your problems."*

That is a true statement. You begin to stop stressing and worrying over your problems because you're helping to make a difference in someone else's life. On the other hand, don't allow other people's problems to become yours either. You help by guiding them towards the right path in a positive manner. When you give your time to help people, that shows spiritual growth, and it gives you courage to continue to walk on the path God has for you. Many times, God allows you to be tested throughout your life just to see your spiritual growth. In the Bible (Luke 16:19-31), there is a story of Lazarus and the rich man. In that story, Lazarus was poor and hungry, and the rich man passed him every day while not acknowledging him. When the rich man died, he lifted up his eyes in hell and from afar he saw Lazarus in heaven while he begged Lazarus for a drip of water to quench his thirst. That story is a great example of reaping what you sow and not giving to the poor. He walked pass Lazarus every day and didn't care to feed him. In return, he needed Lazarus to give him water. That's like the old saying, "Treat people good because you never know who may have to give you a drink of water." God means what He says. You will reap what you sow whether good or bad. Giving out of your abundant from the heart and not complaining is pleasing to God. You will always have what you need and more when you sacrifice for others. Be the giver and inspire someone else to do the same.

FIND YOUR ULTIMATE PURPOSE

*For whom he did foreknow, he also did predestinate
to be conformed to the image of his Son, that he
might be the firstborn among many brethren.*
—Romans 8:29

*Before I formed thee in the belly I knew thee; and
before thou camest forth out of the womb
I sanctified thee, and I ordained thee
a prophet unto the nations.*
—Jeremiah 1:5

We were all created for a purpose, and our lives are predestined. However, many people are still trying to find out their life's purpose. Our ultimate purpose in life is to glorify God in all that we do whether it's in music, politics, etc. From birth, God knew what gifts to give you to help you figure out what you're on earth to do. It's not a coincidence that someone has a gift to hear music and play it or you have a gift to speak in public. Whatever gifts or talents you have are in line with your purpose; and when you realize what your purpose is, you should glorify God through it. We are supposed to praise God and acknowledge Him throughout our lives.

Praise ye the Lord.
Praise God in his sanctuary:
praise him in the firmament of his power.
Praise him for his mighty acts:
praise him according to his excellent greatness.
Praise him with the sound of the trumpet:
praise him with the psaltery and harp.
Praise him with the timbrel and dance:
praise him with stringed instruments and organs.
Praise him upon the loud cymbals:
praise him upon the high sounding cymbals.
Let everything that hath breath praise the Lord.
Praise ye the Lord.
—Psalm 150

We were created to praise and glorify God. Once you realize that the ultimate purpose is to glorify God, you will begin to seek Him more, and He will lead you to your calling. He wants you to acknowledge Him so that He can elevate you to next level of your purpose. In order to find your purpose and for God to use you, there can't be any jealousy, bitterness, guilt, or anger in you. God can't elevate you when you have a lot of mess in you. There can't be room in your mind to seek your purpose when you can't focus. Once you remove the mess from your mind, you can focus and hear from God. Sometimes, in order to hear from God, you have to be still and give Him your full attention. Once you have a clear mind and God has your full attention, everything falls into place. Even when you don't see God working or when you think God is silent, He is shifting things around in your favor.

For the vision is yet for an appointed time,
but at the end it shall speak, and not lie:
though it tarry, wait for it;
because it will surely come, it will not tarry.
—Habakkuk 2:3

If God gave you a vision, then believe that it will come to pass. Many times, we slow ourselves down from reaching our full potential because we allow obstacles to hinder us. The children of Israel are a good example of how obstacles hindered them from getting to the promise land. If they didn't complain and worship idol gods, they would have made it to the promise land in way less time than forty years. Yet, God brought the vision to pass because of His promise. The vision and promise that God has for you have been appointed, but it is up to you to go after it and seek the Lord. It is very sad to see people waste their lives because they don't have a clue what their purpose is. They sit around working on a job that they weren't supposed to work. They allowed obstacles to hinder them from reaching their full potential. Without a vision, you will perish. Satan wants you to perish. He doesn't want to see you find your purpose; He will tempt you to get on the wrong path and lead you to destruction. He will even try to place people in your path to keep you from finding your purpose. That is why it is important that you meditate daily on God's Word and pray. When you pray and ask God to guide you, Satan can't trick you because you will have wisdom to discern things. Prayer changes things, and it shows God that you have faith to acknowledge Him. Life without prayer is meaningless because through prayer is how you communicate with God. When you communicate with God, He can lead you to the purpose He has for you. Many times what you're passionate about has a lot to do with your purpose. For instance, some people are passionate about creating a cure for cancer. Every time they try to do something else, they keep going back to wanting to research on how to find a cure. When you find yourself passionate about something that you can't stop thinking about, your purpose is usually surrounded around your passion. God doesn't put passion in your heart for no reason because He knows that is how you will find your purpose. And, when you seek the Lord, He will take that passion and give you a vision that no man can stop. He will open doors for you to walk into your destiny, and He will place people in your life to help you. All you have to do is trust Him and know that He is in control. You can't stress or worry about getting to the next level of your destiny because His timing is better than yours. He will take you places that you never could imagine, but you have to patient.

And let us not be weary in well doing: for in due season we shall reap, if we faint not.
—Galatians 6:9

Patience is the key to reaching your full potential. God has to prepare you, and He wants you to remain humble. God works through your humility, and many times at your lowest moment you find your purpose. I've heard several stories of people seeking the Lord at their lowest moment in life, which helped them find out what their calling in life is. God allows people to have trials and tribulations to get them on the right track and to keep them on the right track. If you never have trials, you would probably never acknowledge God. He wants you to lean and depend on Him, so that He can bless you and give you the best in life. In seeking your purpose, you will realize that you are created to do wonderful works as Jesus did. Jesus lived His purpose, and He showed us how to lead a righteous life and shun from temptation. He knew He was born to die for the greater good of humanity; and during His life, He performed many miracles. God created us all to do the same. Instead of cursing people, you should bless them and pray for their soul to be saved. When you know your purpose, you will be happy to see other people strive to be the best and reach their full potential. You will encourage others around you and show them that they can do all things through Christ. On the other hand, people who don't know their purpose are lost. They are lost and hopeless, and they don't want to see others be successful. People who live their life without purpose are never satisfied because they always have a void in their heart. They're constantly seeking after things that are not in line with the purpose God has for them. When dealing with people who have not found their purpose, you have to pray for them and help them find out what that burning desire is in their heart. You have to show them how to trust and lean on God.

Trust in the Lord with all thine heart; and lean not unto thine own understanding. In all thy ways acknowledge him, and he shall direct thy paths.
—Proverbs 3:5-6

Trusting and depending on God is the key because He will anoint you and give you favor in life. You have to trust that He knows which direction to take you and what places to lead you too. The Holy Spirit is never wrong, and you have to get to a point in life where you let the Holy Spirit guide you. When God has a purpose and a calling on your life, you can't run from it. Jonah is a prime example of someone who ran from his calling, and he had to go through some obstacles to get back on the right path. God called him to go minister in Nineveh, but Jonah wanted to do it his way and go to another city. On his journey to the other city, God allowed a storm to come, and he was casted into the sea where a fish swallowed him whole. Jonah had to spend three days and three nights in the belly of the fish. During the time while in the belly of the fish, he prayed to God to let him out and God did. When he was released from the fish God called him to go to Nineveh again and he went. If it's meant for you to fulfill a certain purpose, then you can run, but you can't hide. Being disobedient will cause you to go through a lot of turmoil. But, when you obey God and walk in the purpose He designed for your life, He will protect and bless you. You will be so blessed that people around you will be blessed. You have to have faith and know that God will never leave you nor forsake you. He has greater in store for you, and through your purpose you will change the world. You never know who you may have an impact on when you walk in your destiny. Yet, in order to find your purpose; you have to love, forgive, overcome, and give. When you learn how to do those things, you can have a clear mind to hear from God. He can lead you to your destiny. You won't continue to live a depressed and boring life because you will always be looking for more to conquer through your purpose. Seek God first and then your purpose will be revealed unto you; and when you find your purpose, get to work.

GET TO WORK

For thou shalt eat the labour of thine hands: happy shalt thou be, and it shall be well with thee.
—Psalms 128:2

After you find out your purpose in life, you have to apply yourself. God wants you to get to work and exercise your gifts and talents that He gave you. You have to get rid of the spirit of procrastination and just do what God says. You can't complain and sit around waiting for something to happen. There has to be some work put into rising to the level of greatness.

Even so faith, if it hath not works, is dead, being alone. Yea, a man may say, Thou hast faith, and I have works: shew me thy faith without thy works, and I will shew thee my faith by my works.
—James 2: 17-18 KJV

You can have faith and believe that you will reach greatness; but if you don't do anything and ponder around, how do you expect to reach your goals? Procrastinators don't really have faith because when you have faith, you will take a chance to do something without knowing what the outcome may be. You will work and not contemplate on things because you know that God has your best interest. He wants us to be laborers and work hard to uplift His kingdom.

> *Therefore said he unto them, The harvest truly is great, but the labourers are few: pray ye therefore the Lord of the harvest, that he would send forth labourers into his harvest.*
> *—Luke 10:2 KJV*

It is your duty to work and maximize your greatness. God blesses those who work earnestly and trust in Him. Michael Jordan knew from high school that he wanted to play basketball, and even though he didn't make the team, he never stopped working on improving his skills. He did so well that he is still considered one of the greatest basketball players of all time. God blessed him because of the hard work he put into his passion of playing basketball. Hard work never goes unnoticed to God, so don't think your time is wasted. Keep working and walking in the purpose that God has for your life. However, there will be temptations that will come along to take your focus away from your purpose. There will be people trying to distract you from "getting to work" and living in God's greatness; but when you have the gift to discern things, those distractions will go away. Discernment is a key element that people should have in life because without it you will fall for anything. Satan and his workers like to get people off the right path, so they won't live in God's greatness. He wants you to be depressed or jealous so you won't focus on your purpose and get to work to make this world a better place. He knows that He can't have your soul once you've given your life to Christ, but He will do all he can to make you useless and distract you from living in God's greatness. But, when you are hard at work and you're focused on your purpose, nothing will take you off your path. You won't be concerned with others, and you won't worry about obtaining a certain amount of success because your faith is anchored and you know that God will bless you. There won't be any doubt in your spirit about what God can do. From experience, I realize that all the hard work I put into something, and God has blessed me to see the fruits of my labor. Imagine, if everyone in the world found their purpose and walked in it. People would have more joy, and they wouldn't have a reason to be jealous of someone else. God didn't create you to just be here. He wants you to work diligently in the purpose that He has for your life. As much time as many people waste talking about someone else and what they're doing, they could use that time to work on projects that are in line with their purpose. Talking never gets the job done. God wants to see you be active and put your gifts to use. Once you step out on faith and use the gifts He gave you, blessings will flow. Being lazy is a sin because you're not taking the initiative to get to work! How can you expect to get an interview if you didn't apply for a job? You can't be afraid to go after your purpose or afraid to apply yourself. Once you take the initiative and apply that interview or whatever you applied to do, it will happen. Yet, when you are working and walking in your purpose, you should never complain because when you complain you will never excel to the next level. God loves you when you appreciate things as well as being always grateful. If you notice, most people that reach a certain level of success are humble people who are always grateful. God exalts those who are low and meek. Even God Himself came down and humbled Himself in the flesh as Jesus Christ. And, Jesus rode on a donkey to serve others, so if God can do that, then we should be more willing to be humble. Get to work, do it with your whole heart and remain humble.

For even the Son of man came not to be ministered unto, but to minister, and to give his life a ransom for many.
—Mark 10:45 KJV

When God shows you your purpose, you have to remember that He specifically gave that calling to you. It doesn't matter if there are a thousand other people out there working in the same career field as you. You have to remember, "Many are called but few are chosen (Matthew 22:14)," and God has a different purpose for you than anyone else, so don't be concerned with people competing for the same job. When you are chosen by God, there is no such thing as competition. God chooses whom He wants to work and where He wants them to work. You have to continue to walk on the path created for you, and work hard for His kingdom. It is not a coincidence that He gave you the gift to prophesy and then called you to minister to the nation. Just as God created everyone to be different, He created each of us to have a different purpose. On the other hand, some people may think that they're on the right path to their purpose, but they're walking on their own path and not God's path. Like Paul, in the Bible, who persecuted Christians and didn't believe until he met Jesus on the road to Damascus (Acts 9). God had to change his path and renew his mind. Once Paul became a Christian, he shared the Gospel throughout the world until the day he was persecuted. His path had to change in order to work on the building of the kingdom of God. When God calls you, it's your duty to get to work and move in the direction He has prepared for you. God already has the journey mapped out for you, but it's up to you to follow it. Walking on the path God has prepared for you is much easier than walking on your own path. He blesses those who obey Him and acknowledge Him. Even if you feel like things are moving too slowly, you have to trust God and know that He is working. He is always working on your behalf and making sure you are well prepared to work harder when He elevates you to the next level. Hard work and determination leads to living in God's greatness.

The soul of the sluggard desireth, and hath nothing:
but the soul of the diligent shall be made fat.
—Proverbs 13:4 KJV

Living in God's greatness is the best thing you can imagine in this life and the next life. God wants us to prosper in all that we do, and He wants us to reap the benefits of what we sow. Even in heaven, you will reap the benefits of the hard work you've done while living on this earth.

For he that soweth to his flesh shall of the flesh reap corruption; but he that soweth to the Spirit shall of the Spirit reap life everlasting.
—Galatians 6:8 KJV

And, behold, I come quickly; and my reward is with me, to give every man according as his work shall be.
—Revelation 22:12 KJV

God sees your good works, and what you do for His kingdom will last and be well rewarded. A reward from God is much more valuable than a reward from anyone. You will never be able in a lifetime to beat God's giving. Why not prosper on earth as well as in heaven? When you work and walk in the purpose that God has for you, prosperity is always present. God will not withhold anything good from you! I pray you come to an understanding of finding your purpose and working towards building God's kingdom. I pray that you learn to love others and forgive those who may have hurt you (including yourself) because God wants you to do miraculous things in this world. You have to get rid of the hate, jealousy, and guilt to reach your full potential. God teaches us to overcome and give back to those who are less fortunate. Through overcoming obstacles, you will find your calling while God uses that to elevate you to the next level in your life. Remain humble and keep God first in all that you do, and you will be abundantly blessed. Don't allow the devil to tempt you into being jealous, selfish, hateful, unforgiving, and oppressed. Stay focused on working on your purpose and bringing forth fruit, so that you can bless others. Once you take these steps and find your purpose in life, you will begin to live in God's greatness. Everything you touch will be golden, and you will always prosper. There will never be sorrow in what you do. God will always supply what you need, and He will give you the desires of your heart.

PRAYER

Read Out Loud

Dear Lord, I thank You for Your grace and mercy.
I thank You for Your compassion and patience.
I ask that you help me overcome
these obstacles that I face.
Please lead and guide me toward my purpose
to uplift your kingdom.
Lord, forgive me of anything that I have done that
is not pleasing to you.
Cleanse me from all unrighteousness.
Bless me to bless others.
In Jesus name Amen.

www.ingramcontent.com/pod-product-compliance
Lightning Source LLC
Chambersburg PA
CBHW050607300426
44112CB00013B/2111